colour me!

cREATE
YOUR
OWN
calm

Published by Collins
An imprint of HarperCollins Publishers
Westerhill Road, Bishopbriggs,
Glasgow G64 2QT

www.harpercollins.co.uk

978-0-00836758-9

Printed in Slovenia by GPS Group

10 9 8 7 6 5 4 3 2 1

Thanks to Michelle I'Anson, Lauren
Murray, Kevin Robbins, Gordon MacGilp,
Kitty Chivers and all the team at
HarperCollins for championing calmness.
Thank you Clare Forrest for the
magical illustrations.

For Frankie, Annalise, Jasmine, Charlie,
Isaac, Alfie, Jamie, Josh and Luke.
May your lives be filled with peace,
love and adventure.

#CYOCalm

CREATE YOUR OWN CALM

Becky Goddard-Hill

illustrated by Clare Forrest

Sometimes life is exciting and you feel full of bubbles and fizz. The very last thing you want to do is calm down.

At other times – when you are frightened, upset, worried or angry – you might long to feel peaceful but find it hard.

How many times has someone told you to calm down? It doesn't work, does it? Often, it just makes you feel even more wound up.

What you need to know is HOW to calm down and how to do it for yourself.

About this book

This book looks at ways to help you create your own calm with activities such as mindfulness, yoga, nature, art, baking and exercise. It will teach you how to make worry dolls and scented dough. It will help you discover steps to manage your fears and your anger more positively and lots, lots more.

Each topic contains:

- An inspiring quote to motivate you or make you think.

- Science or research that explains how the calming strategy works.

- An activity to help you put what you have learned into practice.

THOUGHTS & FEELINGS

nature

RELATIONSHIPS

WORDS

simplicity

CREATIVITY

MIND & BODY

Each section is full to the brim with handy hints on how you can relax in your everyday life, and in those moments when it all gets too much.

How to use this book

You can work through this book in order or you can dip in and pick any activity you fancy. Rather than read it all at once, you might want to read one topic and have a good go at it before moving on. You may want to involve your grown-up in the book or you may want to keep it private to start with. It's totally up to you.

Some of the activities (like belly breathing, positive affirmations and earthing) might seem a bit unusual at first but I urge you to keep an open mind and give them a go. We never know what will work for us until we give it a try.

Being able to create your own calm is a skill for life and, the sooner you learn how, the more peaceful and happy your life will be.

Have fun!

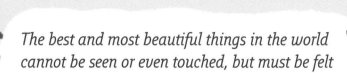

The best and most beautiful things in the world cannot be seen or even touched, but must be felt with the heart.

— Helen Keller (Author and activist)

Your thoughts and feelings are powerful and they ARE something you can control.

If you think, 'Agggh, I'll never get this homework done!' you are likely to FEEL worried and fed up.

BUT

If you think, 'I've done half my homework, the end is in sight' you'll FEEL more confident and optimistic.

This section looks at various thoughts and feelings and shows you how to make them more positive and a lot more helpful.

1. All feelings matter

Always be true to your feelings, because the more you deny what you feel, the stronger it becomes.

— Anonymous

Our feelings have a HUGE effect on how we think and behave and they all matter, even the uncomfortable ones.

If you don't allow yourself to feel all your emotions, they will bubble up and overflow in ways that can feel overwhelming.

If your emotions get too much or they aren't useful, you don't have to act on them. You can just let them pass instead. For example, being too scared about an exam could affect how well you do, being too angry with a friend could ruin a friendship.

You need to learn to recognise the feelings that are useful.

How it works

Scientists at a university in California did an experiment with tarantulas. People who said how they felt about the tarantula (terrified!) were less fearful the next time they saw one than the people who didn't say how they felt.

Scientists believe that naming emotions can help people recognise that they are temporary and that there's a reason for them. This helps them to calm down.

On a sheet of paper, write the following words:

Confused Jealous Happy Sad Irritated Worried Excited Embarrassed Calm Annoyed Peaceful Scared Ashamed Proud Angry AMAZED Shy Bored Anxious

How to play

Cut out each word, fold it in half and put all the pieces of paper in a bowl.

Take it in turns to pull a feeling from the bowl and then describe when you last felt that way.

If you don't want to discuss that feeling you are absolutely allowed to pick again.

Variation: Another way to play is to say what MIGHT make you feel that way. For example, if I picked ANGRY, I could say that someone pinching my bike might make me feel that way.

The point of the game is to help you explore how you feel and to make you more comfortable expressing how you feel to somebody else.

This is called emotional literacy.

Create your own calm...

...by learning to name how you feel.

2. Catastrophising

I am an old man and have known a great many troubles, but most of them never happened.
                                    - Mark Twain (Author)

Do you react to things in dramatic ways, even when they aren't big things? Do you get yourself upset because you have lost your pencil case or because someone didn't pick you first in a game?

It's normal to feel upset when something happens that we don't like, but when we have a big reaction to something small, this is called catastrophising (cat-astro-fi-sing).

Lots of people do this and it causes them worry and stress. It can feel out of your control but it absolutely isn't – you can change this.

It is important to be able to be clear about what is just a small blip and what is genuinely a big problem.

How it works

In one study, researchers asked dental patients to make a note of the thoughts and images that came up in their minds during a stressful dental treatment. They found that patients who had negative thoughts suffered higher levels of pain than those who did not.

How we think about things makes a difference.

How to stop catastrophising

- Talk your worry over with someone who you know is sensible. They can help you see things differently.

- Calm yourself down before looking at what's wrong. You'll approach the issue far less emotionally.

- Look at the facts rather than how you feel. It will help you get perspective.

Activity: Work out what matters

Have a go at ranking these issues in order of their 'catastrophe' rating, starting with the lowest (give it a 1) and the highest (give it a 10).

1. The school holidays are cancelled.

2. You lose your lunch box.

3. You have to miss playing the lead role in the school play because you are ill.

4. Someone is bullying you.

5. Your mum tells you off for not getting ready on time.

6. The hairdresser cuts your hair too short.

7. You aren't picked for the football team.

8. Your best friend has a sleepover at someone else's house.

9. It is raining and you wanted to go to the park.

10. It really is the end of the world.

1 _____

2 _____

3 _____

4 _____

5 _____

6 _____

7 _____

8 _____

9 _____

10 _____

Now look at the list again.

Is there something you can do in each scenario to make the situation better? Sometimes you just need to let things go, but often there is something you can do to ease things.

Create your own calm...

...by getting some perspective on what actually matters.

3. Fear

The fears we don't face become our limits.

- Anonymous

There are two types of fear: instinctive fears and conditioned fears.

Instinctive fears are fears we are born with and these keep us safe. They include things like fear of falling or of fire. These fears are useful!

Conditioned fears usually come about after one bad experience that makes us afraid of something similar happening again. Perhaps you once got sick in a toilet at school and now you won't go to the toilet at school (even though you KNOW it only happened once). These fears can become problems.

Avoiding the things you fear doesn't get rid of them, it just keeps the fear alive and makes it bigger in your mind.

How it works

Scientists have found out that we can smell fear and that it is catching!

They got a group of men to watch a scary film and then asked a group of women (who didn't know about the scary film) to smell their sweat. The smell of the men's fear made them fearful too.

Fear stinks!

So, if you are facing something you are scared of, you need calm and confident people around you (who don't smell of FEAR!).

A good way to get over a fear is to face it step by step. This is called exposure therapy.

Activity: Conquer your fears

Think of something you are a bit frightened of (not something you are absolutely terrified of – let's start small).

If it were me, I would choose mice.

Because I am a bit frightened of mice, I avoid them. My friend has a pet mouse and it means I don't visit her. This means I never get the chance to see that they aren't that scary.

So, here is my plan to increase my exposure to mice so that I can beat my fear:

1. I am going to visit my friend who has a pet mouse and sit in the same room as it.

2. On the second visit, I am going to look at it in its cage for 30 seconds.

3. On my next visit, I am going to look at the mouse in its cage for 2 minutes.

4. The following visit, I am going to gently stroke its head as my friend holds it.

Step by step I will increase my closeness to the mouse and decrease my fear.

Could you make a plan like this (perhaps with help from an adult) to get you closer to what you are scared of?

What would your steps look like? Can you write them in the staircase?

Create your own calm...

...by tackling your fears step by step.

4. How to handle your anger

The greatest remedy for anger is delay.
- Seneca (Roman philosopher)

Anger is not an emotion you have to avoid. Feelings are just feelings, they are not who you are, and they will pass.

What you need to be more aware of is how you behave in your anger.

Yes, it's right to stand up for the kid who's being bullied, BUT if you act in anger then you may be in trouble too.

How it works

Scientists have discovered that when we feel angry, our intelligence level drops by 30 percent – so we aren't thinking very clearly!

While you're feeling very angry, making decisions about what to do is not a good idea.

You need to relax a little first.

A calm down kit is a collection of things designed to distract and relax you.

Here are a few ideas:

- A joke book (to make you laugh)
- A bottle of bubbles and some feathers (for you to practise slow breathing)
- A notebook and pen (for you to empty your mind and express the things that are bothering you)
- A stress ball you can squeeze and release (to decrease muscle tightness)
- A skipping rope (so you can get tension out of your body)
- An MP3 player with some relaxing music on it (to bring your heart rate down)
- A bottle of baby oil (so you can give yourself a hand massage)

Create your own calm...

...by dealing with your angry feelings in a positive way.

5. Faulty thinking

If you change the way you look at things, the things you look at change.
- Wayne Dyer (Motivational speaker)

Faulty thoughts (also called cognitive distortions) are ways of thinking that convince you to believe something that isn't true.

How it works

Psychiatrist Aaron T. Beck (who discovered faulty thinking) believes that once we spot these negative thought patterns, we can challenge them. Here are some examples:

- All-or-nothing thinking is when you see something as only good or bad. For example, you play well in a piano concert apart from missing a couple of notes. Saying it was a disaster is all-or-nothing thinking. You can miss out on lots of lovely feelings when you think like this.

- Fortune telling is when you think you know what will happen in the future and usually imagine the worst. You might assume that no one will want to be your friend in your new scout group, so you decide not to go. But you don't know how things will work out till you try, so it's much better to put on your friendliest smile and give it a go.

- Mind reading is when you think you know what someone is thinking without asking them. For example, your friend may not want to play, so you assume he dislikes you (whereas he might be sad because his dog is ill). It is always important to ask and check facts rather than try and mind read.

- Generalising is when you believe that because something happened once, it will happen again. For example, you might believe every cat will scratch you because it happened once before. Generalising doesn't make something true.

Create your own calm...

...by challenging any faulty thoughts you have.

6. Worrying

That the birds of worry and care fly over your head, you cannot change. But that they build nests in your hair, this you can prevent.

- Chinese proverb

Letting your worries hang around too long (building nests in your hair) will make you feel rubbish.

Everyone feels anxious or worried from time to time. It is quite normal in certain situations such as tests, going to a new school or trying out for a play.

Sometimes worrying is useful. It can remind us to revise, to try hard and to prepare.

But worrying is a problem if it happens all the time, keeps you awake, makes your body tense and takes your time and energy away from other, good things.

Let's look at how to tackle that.

How it works

A study at the University of Pennsylvania encouraged people who worried a lot to do these four things:

1. Identify exactly what you are worrying about.
2. Decide on a time to think about it.
3. Distract yourself if you are worrying at other times.
4. At 'worry time', think of solutions to the worry rather than about the worry itself.

Worry time

For example, you might go for a jog or a walk in the park. While you're there, you can go over everything that's on your mind and then, when you're finished, you can stop worrying and focus on your day.

Having a specific 'worry time' means worries aren't always bugging you and you can get on with happier things.

When could your worry time be?

Keep a worry box or journal

When worries pop up, it can help to write them down and get them out of your head. A journal is a great place to do this, or you could write your worry on a slip of paper and place it in a worry box.

The box or journal will hold you worries for you so you don't have to think about them until you are ready. Then, at a specific time (your worry time) you can look at them again and consider what to do.

You will need:

- An old shoe box or tissue box
- PVA glue
- Colouring pens
- Stickers
- Paper or card

You might want to use the colouring pens and stickers to decorate your box like a worry-eating monster. You can make hair or arms out of the paper or card and use your glue to stick these on. It's totally up to you.

Whenever you start to worry about something, write it on a slip of paper and put it in your worry box.

Create your own calm...

...by managing your worries so they don't take up too much space in your life.

7. The negativity bias

Keep your face always toward the sunshine, and shadows will fall behind you.

- Walt Whitman (Poet)

Did you know your brain has something called a 'negativity bias'? This means that you are more likely to give time and attention to negative things than positive ones.

It's why we often remember being told off more than praised and why we remember bad times more than good times. It is thought that our brains work like this because, in prehistoric times, if we paid more attention to danger we were more likely to survive!

Times have changed though, and you can change your brain to behave differently through repeated actions and choices that we make.

IMAGINE

How it works

The ability to train and adapt our brains is down
to something amazing called neuroplasticity.

PEACE

In a study on positive thinking, 90 students
were split into two groups. The first group
wrote about a positive experience each day
for three days in a row. The second group
wrote about something else. Three months later,
the students who wrote about positive experiences
had better moods and fewer illnesses.

HUG

BREAthE

Activity: Positive thinking

cALM

For the next three days, sit down and write
about what has been awesome about your
day. If you enjoy doing this, you might make
it a daily practice.

REST

FRIENd

If you don't like writing, that's okay – instead you
could TELL a grown-up about all the good things
that have happened.

Create your own calm...

RELAX

stiLL

...by changing your brain to focus more
on the positive things in life.

NURTURE

8. Problem-solving

The best way out is always through.
— Robert Frost (Poet)

From time to time we all have problems and sometimes they weigh heavy on our minds. What matters isn't the problem, it's how we respond to it. It is really helpful to be a good problem-solver.

How it works

A 2010 study found that kids who lack problem-solving skills are more likely to be depressed, and that learning problem-solving skills can improve young people's mental health.

Activity: Be a problem-solver

First, divide any worries you may have into the columns below:

Things I can control	Things I can't control

With the things you can't control, you are just going to have to accept there is nothing you can do and try and make your peace with the situation.

Let's look at the things you can control... pick the problem that you want to tackle first.

1. You need to be crystal clear about what your problem actually is. Write it down.

2. Come up with ideas for ways to solve your problem.

3. Decide which one you want to try out, then devise a plan of action. What can you do, how are you going to do it and when?

4. Put your plan into action!

5. If it didn't quite work, dust yourself off, start again from step 1 and devise a new plan. If it did work, celebrate your awesome problem-solving skills.

A problem-solving mindset is useful – it turns a problem into a challenge that you CAN overcome.

Create your own calm...

...by taking a step-by-step approach to tackling your problems.

9. Fight or flight

Nothing can bring you peace but yourself.
— Ralph Waldo Emerson (Writer)

When people were faced with dangerous animals in prehistoric times, they could either fight or run away. It was a matter of survival.

You rarely come across sabre-toothed tigers these days but your body sometimes acts like you do when you feel anxious or worried.

This feeling is called the 'fight or flight response'.

It can be triggered by something real such as a falling tree, in which case running away is SMART. But, more often, it is triggered by things you feel anxious about such as a test at school or a dog in the park.

Your brain reacts as if you're in danger, whether the danger is real or not.

How it works

The amygdala is the part of our brain responsible for our emotions. When we are very stressed or scared, it passes a message to the control centre of our brain which immediately sends warning signals around the body. These signals cause adrenaline to be released and this gets us ready to either fight or run away.

When adrenaline is released, your muscles tense, your heart beats faster and your breathing speeds up. You might sweat and tremble too. Your body is telling your brain that, yes, there is something to be frightened of.

But don't worry, you can make it stop by calming your brain and your body down in just two simple steps.

Step 1 - calming your brain

If you express your feelings out loud, write them down or just say them to yourself, this will calm your brain down and you will be able to think more clearly.

Step 2 - calming your body

Calming your body down is simple too. Breathing deeply brings more oxygen into your lungs and helps slow your heart rate. This change in your body tells your brain there is nothing to be afraid of and all is well.

Try breathing in for a count of 5 then slowly breathing out for a count of 5. Do this five times or more until it works.

Activity

In the space on the next page, draw your body and label what you feel when it's in fight or flight mode.

Try and write a comment next to each area of your body.

Create your own calm...

...by identifying your feelings and breathing deeply.

draw yourself
here

↓

10. Venting

Angry people are not always wise.
                              - Jane Austen (Writer)

Venting is when you let out all of your frustrations and anger. People who are upset often just want to be heard so when you are venting you might repeat your story (a lot). But sometimes you will vent because it can seem safer and easier than dealing with the problem. It can be helpful or unhelpful, depending on how you do it.

Helpful venting

It can feel good to let bottled-up feelings out and release tension by telling them to a friend.

Knowing you are understood and cared about may help you calm down a little too.

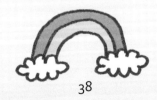

Unhelpful venting

Venting doesn't necessarily change the situation though, and the person you vent to may eventually get fed up of being your dumping-ground.

If you vent on the person who upset you they might get very emotional and attack you back, then you could end up feeling worse.

How it works

A 2013 study found that people who regularly ranted on the internet were more likely to develop anger-management problems. The study concluded that the more we rant, the angrier we get.

That doesn't mean we shouldn't express how we feel and let our feelings out though. Psychiatrists have been advising us to do this for a long time. But it does mean we shouldn't give LOTS of time and energy to ranting, because that can make things worse.

How to vent in a positive way

If you are venting to a friend, choose someone you trust not to gossip or just agree with everything you say. Keep it short and don't repeat yourself.

If you want to vent to the person who has upset you and feel it would be helpful, it is a good idea to calm yourself down first. You can do this through exercise, relaxation or distraction. Try and express your feelings rather than launch an attack. Then, make sure you listen to the other person too. Move quickly on to the 'What can we do about this to make it better?' stage.

Activity: Healthy venting

Is there something you want to vent? Writing it down might be a good way to get it clear in your mind. Have a good vent in the speech bubble on the opposite page about something that's making you upset.

Has getting it out felt good and are you glad you wrote it rather than said it?

Create your own calm...

...by venting in healthy ways and calming yourself down first.

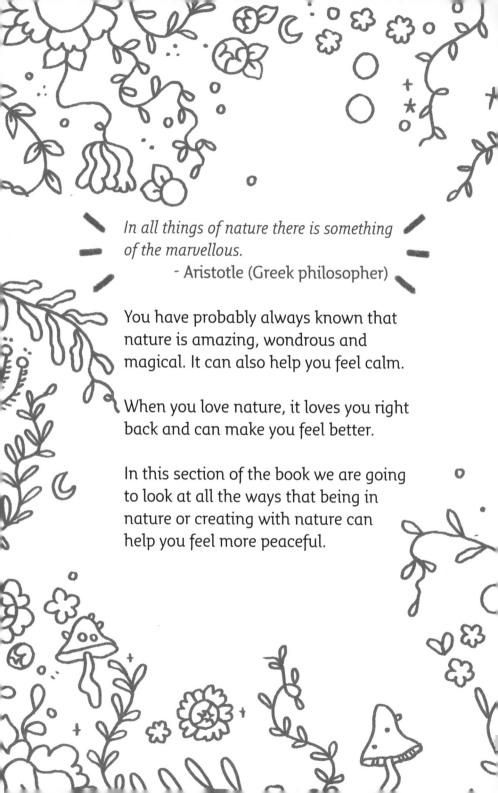

In all things of nature there is something of the marvellous.

— Aristotle (Greek philosopher)

You have probably always known that nature is amazing, wondrous and magical. It can also help you feel calm.

When you love nature, it loves you right back and can make you feel better.

In this section of the book we are going to look at all the ways that being in nature or creating with nature can help you feel more peaceful.

nature

colour me

11. Nature crafts

In crafting there are no mistakes, just unique creations.
- Anonymous

Making art and crafts from nature is a wonderful way to relax. Just let go of the idea of perfection and focus on your creation being uniquely yours.

How it works

Scientists have discovered that the average person has 60,000 thoughts per day.

Our poor busy brains!

Often when we are doing something creative, we find ourselves in what's known as a state of 'flow'. This focuses the mind and lets it take a rest from all that thinking.

Being creative is calming. Nature, we know, also helps people feel calmer. Put the two together and it is doubly powerful.

It can be great fun to create little pieces of art in nature and leave them for others to stumble across. It's like leaving a little gift.

Activity: Make a nature craft window

Collect 4 sticks roughly the same size to use as a frame. Make a square with the sticks then fill the inside with flowers and leaves, stones and shells or whatever natural things you can find to make into a picture.

Here are some more nature art ideas... maybe you have some of your own?

- Make a little picture out of pebbles and leave it on a path – a heart shape is easy
- Create a nature spiral with leaves, sticks, flowers and stones
- Build a stone tower sculpture
- Use daisy chains to decorate a park bench
- Collect conkers and make a giant butterfly outline in the grass

Create your own calm...

...by leaving a little piece of nature art to be found.

12. Cloud watching

When we feel stuck we should look at the sky.
The clouds remind us that everything changes.

— Anonymous

Did you know that the Cloud Appreciation Society has 35,000 members in over 100 countries around the world?

Taking a moment to watch the clouds roll by can bring you an instant hit of calm.

Clouds are awesome in another way too. If you think of your tricky and uncomfortable thoughts and feelings as clouds you will realise they too change and finally float away.

How it works

In one study scientists used some tricky maths challenges to make people anxious. Afterwards, half the group then chilled out in a room with white light, while the other half relaxed in a room with blue light. Those in the room with blue light de-stressed THREE times faster!

Staring up at the blue sky and watching the clouds when you are stressed is a speedy route to chilling out.

How to cloud watch

You can simply pause, focus your attention on the clouds passing by and wonder at how awe-inspiring nature is. This will help you feel part of something bigger and your worries seem smaller.

Or you can let your imagination turn those clouds into pictures – maybe you can see a fire-breathing dragon, a boat or a caterpillar?

Activity: Find a story in the clouds

Find a friend or family member to come and cloud watch with you. Try and empty your mind of anything worrying you and focus on the clouds. Share with each other the pictures you can see.

Can you link your cloud creations together and come up with a crazy story?

Create your own calm...

...by giving cloud watching a try.

13. Lavender playdough

Don't hurry, don't worry. And be sure to smell the flowers along the way.

— Walter Hagen (Golfer)

Scent can be very powerful. It can bring back memories, make you feel excited, make you feel icky or make you feel hungry.

It can also work wonders to help you feel calm.

How it works

A recent study by scientists in Japan showed how lavender can reduce anger, aggression and restlessness.

It works as an anxiolytic (an anxiety reliever), a sedative (to help us sleep) and it helps us relax.

Have a go at making lavender playdough (ask your grown-up to help) and see if the scent relaxes you.

Activity: Make your own lavender playdough

You will need:

- 8 tbsp plain flour
- 2 tbsp table salt
- 60 ml warm water
- Purple food colouring
- 1 tbsp vegetable oil
- Lavender flower heads or lavender oil

1. Mix the flour and salt in a large bowl.

2. In a separate bowl, mix together the water, a few drops of purple food colouring and the oil.

3. Pour the coloured water into the flour mix and combine.

4. Dust a work surface with a little flour and turn out the mixture. Knead together to form a smooth dough.

5. Add some chopped up lavender flower heads and a few drops of lavender oil.

6. Knead the dough some more. It should release a lovely smell as you do. Be sure to wash your hands well afterwards.

7. Store the dough in a plastic box to keep it fresh.

Create your own calm...

...with relaxing, natural scents.

14. Earth Day

*We do not inherit the Earth from our ancestors;
we borrow it from our children.*
- Native American proverb

Earth Day began in 1970 in the USA and is
celebrated on 22nd April each year. It is a day
to think about our planet and what we can do
to keep it healthy.

Did you know...

...that 1 billion people in 192 countries now take part
in celebrating Earth Day each year? It is the biggest
day of environmental action in the whole world.

It's absolutely the greatest party on Earth!

How it works

The American Psychiatric Association says a huge
amount of research has been done that shows
being in nature has a big impact on how calm
people feel and on their emotional health.

Not only is Earth Day about making our Earth feel
better, it works to make us feel better too.

Here are some ways to celebrate Earth Day:

- Camp out in your garden
- Make a blossom picture and display it in your window
- Make a bird feeder
- Go for a family walk
- Catch rainwater and add petals to make perfume!
- Draw a HUGE picture of Earth and fill it with rainbows, animals, sunshine and stars

Activity: Devise a nature treasure hunt

Send out your teams in pairs, with a list of things to hunt for, and tell them the boundary lines of the area they can search. The rules are that nothing can be picked. It should all be found. Here are some suggestions of 'treasure' they could look for:

1. A stone
2. A small stick
3. A pine cone
4. A conker
5. A blade of grass
6. A daisy
7. A piece of litter
8. Some bark
9. A flower
10. A feather

Create your own calm...

...by celebrating Earth Day.

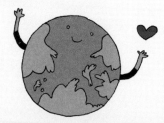

15. Water

Water is the driving force in nature.
                - Leonardo da Vinci (Artist and inventor)

Did you know that 70 percent of our Earth is covered by water? About 60 percent of your body is made up of water too. Without drinking it we could not survive for more than three days.

Water is important for both your body and your mind.

How it works

Scientists know, through many studies, that water helps people feel calm in lots of different ways.

In the water droplets on the opposite page are ways in which water can help you feel calm – can you try them?

Create your own calm...

...by using water to help you cool down.

Drinking between 6–8 glasses of fluid a day is good for both your physical and mental health.

Try watching the rain through your window and let your mind relax to its steady beat.

Swimming helps you stretch your muscles and get into the moment.

A quick shower and a good scrub can give you energy when you are feeling low.

Staring at the sea can fill you with awe, wonder and a sense of peace.

Dancing in the rain and splashing in puddles can lighten your mood no matter what age you are.

When you cry, you are expressing your feelings, which makes you feel so much better than bottling them up does.

Splashing water on your face and wrists when you feel cross or upset helps you cool down.

A long, warm bath can help you feel relaxed and eases tension in your body.

16. Earthing

And forget not that the earth delights to feel your bare feet and the winds long to play with your hair.
- Khalil Gibran (Writer)

Earth is amazing – we can sit on it, stand on it, lay on it, walk on it, run on it and cycle on it. We can find treasures within it, build on it and grow things in it.

Most of the time, due to shoes, we don't come into direct contact with the earth and some people believe this affects our wellbeing.

When we make direct contact with the surface of the earth (through water, sand, grass or soil) with our bare feet or hands, this is called earthing.

How it works

Research on earthing suggests that the impact on the body takes place within 4 seconds as our tense muscles begin to relax and our nervous systems calm down. After 30 minutes, tension and stress are reduced even more.

Some people practise earthing indoors by plugging in special earthing mats, but it isn't necessary to do it that way. You just need to get outside and go barefoot. Did you know that the soles of your feet have over 20,000 nerve endings?

Activity: Connect with the earth

One of the best ways to practise earthing is to walk barefoot on the grass or soil or on the sand.

Do this somewhere you trust not to have broken glass or dog poo! Gardens are good for this.

Note how you feel...

- After 4 seconds of earthing
- After 30 minutes of earthing
- After you sleep that night

Not everyone is convinced that earthing works but it is good to give things a try.

Create your own calm...

...by taking off your shoes and wiggling your toes in the grass.

17. Gardening

To nurture a garden is to feed not just the body, but the soul.

> *- Alfred Austin (Poet and journalist)*

It is hard to be worrying about the past or stressing about the future when you are gardening.
Studying a tiny worm wiggling, or breathing in the scent of home-grown tomatoes, are great ways to feel more peaceful.

Being absorbed in what's happening NOW is called being mindful and it helps you clear your mind and deeply relax.

clAy

cOMpoST

How it works

Scientists found that being outside raises vitamin D levels in our bodies and this, as well as the light from being outside, triggers a positive boost in our moods.

One Dutch study found that people who gardened for 30 minutes had lower cortisol (stress) levels in their bodies than people who read indoors.

It's really good to garden.

seeds

wAteR

Activity: Grow a pizza garden

This is great fun because you get to cook and eat what you grow.

You don't need a lot of space, just some soil and an area you can call your own – perhaps a window box, tub container or a corner of your garden.

If you don't have the space, why not ask at school if you can do this as a class project?

You will need:

- Soil
- Tomato plants
- Basil
- Oregano
- Peppers

You can grow the plants from seed or you can buy small plants (plug plants) that have already started growing.

1. If you're growing the plants from seed, follow the instructions on the seed packet for getting them started.

2. Once your seedlings are big enough, or if you are using plants you have bought, add enough soil to your container so that there is space at the top for planting the plants.

3. Take your plants carefully out of their pots and if you can see the roots, gently ease them apart.

4. Place your plants in the container on top of the soil, and space them out so they have room to grow.

5. Once you have placed your plants, add more soil around the roots, making sure to cover all the roots and fill in the spaces between the plants. Pat the soil down gently but firmly so that your plants are upright and secure.

6. Put your container somewhere sunny and water your plants regularly.

7. If you have lots of space, you could even try making your planting LOOK like a pizza – you simply make a circle out of stones in the soil then divide the area up into 'pizza slice' wedges using string. Plant the different pizza ingredients in each 'slice'.

Create your own calm...

...by growing and eating your own food.

Kind words can be short and easy to speak, but their echoes are truly endless.
> \- Mother Teresa (Nun and missionary)

Words – whether read, written, said aloud or in your head – all have the power to change how you feel.

This section will show you lots of ways to use words to make a difference.

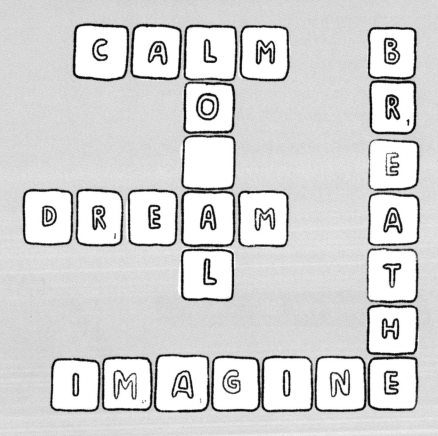

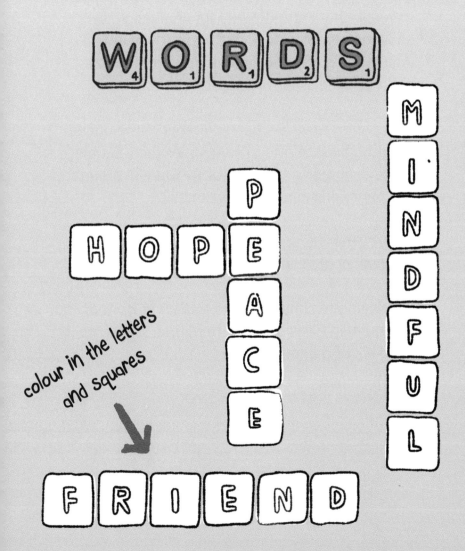

colour in the letters and squares

18. Assertive you

Speak your mind even if your voice shakes.
        - Eleanor Roosevelt (American activist)

Being passive is when you just let things happen to you without standing up for yourself. It is allowing someone to shove in front of you in a queue and saying nothing. Being passive can make you feel frustrated and weak.

Being aggressive is when you react to the queue-jumping by shouting in someone's face. People may see you as a troublemaker. You will probably feel angry, upset and out of control.

Assertiveness is saying what you want and what you feel, politely and firmly.

It is saying to someone who pushes in front of you in a queue, 'I was queuing here first, please go to the back of the line'.

It is always best to be assertive.

You can't always get what you want and need by being assertive but you will be MUCH MORE likely to.

Sometimes being assertive is about saying no. It can be hard to say no to your friends / grown-ups, but if what someone is asking you to do is wrong then you need to keep saying no until they hear you. Sometimes it won't work and then you need to get an adult to help you.

How it works

Studies have shown that assertive people tend to be less anxious than others and it is believed this is because when we are assertive, our frustrations are relieved and are less likely to develop into anxiety or aggression.

Assertive people do these two things:

- They speak in a calm, strong voice
- They express what they feel and what they want to happen

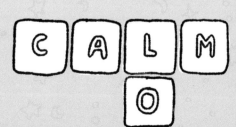

Activity: Assertiveness role plays

Here are some scenarios for you to role play. You could do this with a parent/friend/cuddly toy or even your hamster.

Imagine...

Your dad says you must tidy your room, practise your piano, call grandma and make tea. But you have a HUGE amount of homework to do.

You could say...

I have a lot of homework and that feels too much. I would like to call grandma and tidy my room tomorrow instead.

You have said what you want to happen and expressed your feelings. You have also been polite.

What could you say in these situations? Practise role playing these and write down an assertive response below.

Your friend says you have to carry her school bag because it is too heavy for her.

Your teacher asks you to feed the hamster for the tenth time in a row.

Your cousin wants to play football on the games console but you are tired.

Once you start to find assertiveness easy in your role play you can start to use it in your everyday life. It might be tricky and uncomfortable at first but keep practising and it will soon be easier.

Create your own calm...

...by being assertive – it will make you feel calmer and more in control.

19. Reading

Reading brings us unknown friends.
                    - Honoré de Balzac (Writer)

If you love to read, you will already know how amazingly powerful a book can be. It can educate you, distract you, change your mood and transport you to another world.

But if you have not (yet) discovered the magic of reading, perhaps you just need some tips to help you.

How it works

Reading is a powerful way to relax. Even six minutes can be enough to reduce your stress levels by more than two thirds, according to new research at the University of Sussex. They believe this is because the distraction of entering a whole new world eases tension in both the heart and in our muscles.

Reading works faster than other ways of de-stressing such as listening to music, going for a walk or having a warm drink.

5 tips to help you fall in love with books

1 Try a type of book you haven't read before. So, if serious books make you groan, try a joke book or something more light-hearted. Maybe you like books about people your age, or maybe mysteries will hook you? Generally, the kinds of things you like to watch on TV or at the movies are probably going to be the kinds of books you like to read.

2 Read regularly. Like anything at all that you try, the more you practise the easier it gets. Try 15 minutes a day for a week and see how you go.

3 Try reading a series. It's a great way to get into reading and brilliant to see the same characters across several books. Here are a few you might like:

The Worst Witch
Diary of a Wimpy kid
The Famous Five
The Magic Faraway Tree books
Beast Quest
Ruby Redfort
Murder Most Unladylike
Percy Jackson
Harry Potter

4. Not everyone finds reading easy or fun but pretty much everyone loves a story. Audiobooks are spoken books and they can be a lovely way to help you chill out.

5. Reading should be done somewhere where you can properly relax. Maybe you can read under your duvet with a torch, in a warm bubble bath, or lying on a blanket in the grass. Make your reading space comfy and you will soon get lost in a book.

Activity: book bingo

Book bingo is a great way to read different things. Colour in the tasks on the bingo card as you do them and, when your book bingo is complete, reward yourself with a prize (like a kitchen disco?).

Read a comic or magazine.

Read a recipe and give it a go!

Read a mystery or adventure story!

Swap a book with a friend and read their book!

Ask an adult to recommend a book from their childhood.

Read a book your teacher recommends.

Read a story about an animal!

Read a poem!

Get a book from the library.

Create your own calm...

...by escaping into a story.

20. Word stones

A drop of ink may make a million think.
- George Gordon Byron (Poet)

Words and images are super powerful, aren't they?

You can sprinkle peaceful thoughts throughout the world by writing calming words on stones and spreading them throughout your neighbourhood.

Imagine someone's delight when they find one, and how the calm words and images you have painted will impact their day and everyone they meet.

How it works

Scientists have found that our brains are wired to notice more of what we are thinking about. As you write the calm words on the stone, YOU will feel calmer and be able to think of more ways to relax.

And when other people see the stones the words you have used will grab their attention and they will focus more on calm and serene things in their lives too. Everyone benefits!

Activity: Spread the word

You will need:

- A pebble or smooth stone
- Paint, pens or markers
- Clear varnish (optional)

Simply decorate your stone with your word and once the paint is dry varnish over it to seal it. Do use newspaper on your surface and an apron too!

You could use words like chill, relax, breathe, peace, Zen, serenity. Can you think of more words meaning calm?

Once it's dry, place your stone out in your community for someone to find.

Create your own calm...

...by focusing on peaceful words.

draw your word stone here

21. Peaceful protest

Do your little bit of good where you are; it's those little bits of good put together that overwhelm the world.
- Desmond Tutu (South African human rights activist)

Sometimes you may feel angry or extremely sad about the state of the world. Worries about how animals are treated, climate change, rubbish and poverty can get you down. There are things in our world that are unfair, unkind and worrying.

But feeling helpless never helps.

How it works

Child psychologist Steve Biddulph says that being involved in activism has real mental health benefits. Research indicates that young people involved in taking action and speaking up about causes they believe in report greater levels of happiness and fulfilment than kids who don't.

Activity: Make a peaceful protest

Here are some ideas. You could:

- Join a protest march (with your grown-ups).

- Make a poster and display it in your window/school.

- Write an article about your issue and send it to First News or National Geographic Kids.

- Raise money for the cause you believe in with a sponsored event like a cake sale at school.

- Write to your local MP and ask them to talk to the Government about it.

- Learn about the issue you care about so you can properly tell other people about it.

- Organise an event such as a mass litter pick and get others involved.

Create your own calm...

...by standing up, speaking out and peacefully protesting for causes you care about.

22. Positive affirmations

You are enough just as you are.
                                    - Meghan Markle

Do you have a voice in your head that tells you that you can't do stuff?

If you do, tell that voice to SHUT UP and GET LOST.

This unhelpful voice needs to be replaced with a helpful voice that cheers you on and encourages you. So, if you usually think, 'I am rubbish at maths' you could replace that thought with 'I am getting better at maths with every lesson'.

How it works

Neuroscience shows that by focusing on positive thoughts repeatedly we can change and shape our brains to be more positive. Scientific studies have also shown that both stress and worry can be reduced with positive affirmations.

Activity: Practise positivity

Think about some things you would like to believe about yourself or some that you know are true then turn them into 'I' statements.

For example:

- I feel full of energy and my body is strong
- I am a good friend. I am funny and loyal
- I am a kind and loving person

Make a list of a few that sound good to you. Then, pick one affirmation and practise saying it out loud 5 times each day whilst looking in the mirror. A great time to do this is whilst brushing your teeth.

Try this for a week and see if you feel any different.

 Write yours here

Create your own calm...

...by telling yourself how wonderful you are.

23. The power of words

Better than a thousand useless words is one word that gives peace.

- Buddha

Words are amazingly powerful: they can hurt us, help us, lift us up, put us down, make us do things (or not) and cause us to feel a certain way.

Words have a big, powerful impact on people.

We can use this to our advantage by choosing to speak and focus on words that help us feel good. Complete the word search on the next page to help you focus on being calm.

Create your own calm...

...by using words that change your mood.

Hidden words

```
r e l a x a b t s r c n
e v t m e l l i t s o n
s w e l e b t n r q n a
t e i a h m s e d p f t
z u u c t w e n c a i u
y h q t a t e k i l d r
e e x i e i g e n t l e
z i v a r e p e i m n e
y w n f b u e e n n t t
g h u g a r a n g t o i
l o y a l j c n i r a n
i m a g i n e c t a n u
```

rest	gentle	breathe
quiet	hug	friend
relax	imagine	calm
still	loyal	unite
nature	peace	

No road is long with good company.
                        - Turkish Proverb

Relationships with other people have a huge effect on how you feel. If your relationships are happy and positive, you enjoy them.

If the relationships you have are complicated, full of arguments or uncomfortable, life can feel tough.

This section of the book explores how you can make your relationships with others run smoothly and bring you more happiness and peace.

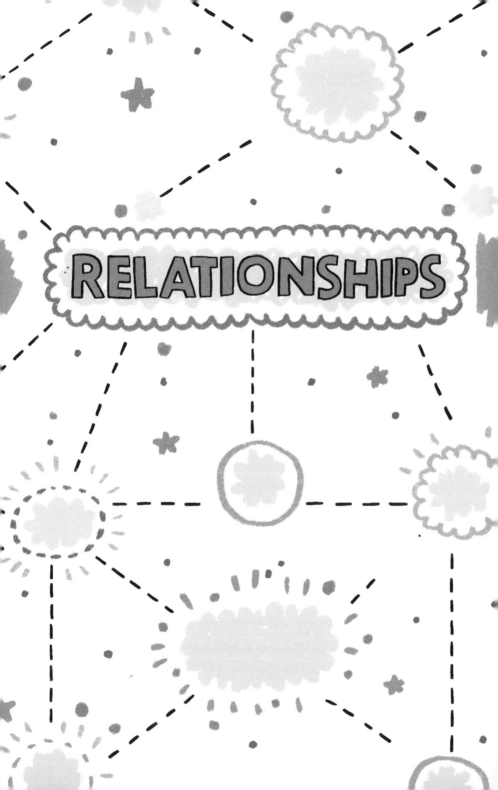

RELATIONSHIPS

24. Calm at home

Home is where your story begins.
                              - Unknown

How peaceful your home is will have a huge impact on you. Does your sister annoy you? Do you fall out with your mum and dad?

Well, you can't control everything in life and you certainly can't control other people.

BUT

You CAN control yourself and the way you react to things. There are some simple things you can do to make family life less stressful.

How it works

Research examining 5,000 young people has shown that when children eat with their parents regularly, they are more likely to be emotionally strong and have better mental health. It was also shown that parents that eat with their families have less stress too.

The evidence is clear: if you sit down with your family to eat regularly, home will be calmer.

Siblings

Your siblings know you better than anyone and they also know how to wind you up better than anyone. They may get jealous of sharing you with your parents and they may take their bad moods out on you.

So, what you can you do?

Well, you can try and be an amazing sibling. In any relationship, you usually get what you give.

Try these two things over the next 7 days and see if it makes a difference to your relationship:

1   Support them – cheer them on in a sports match or wish them good luck in a test.
2   Do fun things with them, like playing board games or watching a funny movie.

You might well be amazed at the impact of these small actions.

Parents

Parents can be annoying, can't they? They tell you to tidy your room, do your homework, do this, don't do that. It can lead to lots of arguing.

If you and your parents get stuck on something, try and negotiate so both of you are (mostly) happy. This is called 'finding the middle ground'.

For example, if they want you to miss a school disco because they think you have too much homework, perhaps you could agree to get up early the next morning to get it finished instead?

Try looking for a win-win rather than arguing.

And what about chores? Well, to be fair, if you just do them your parents won't need to nag.

Activity: Your happy place

Having a place to go in your home that is calm and relaxing is helpful for times when you need some space from your family. Draw your happy place in the frame on the next page.

MY HAPPY PLACE

Create your own calm...

...by being a positive, problem-solving family member who has a happy place to run to if it all gets too much.

25. Calm in the world

I am a part of all that I have met.
                    - Alfred Tennyson (Poet)

We are all connected to each other and to our Earth, and how we behave makes an impact. Respect and kindness lead to a calmer, healthier Earth and calmer, happier people.

The tale of the blue-haired lady

Let me tell you a story about my daughter Annalise...

One day standing in a queue waiting to be served by a woman who just looked FURIOUS WITH LIFE, my little girl beamed up at her and said, 'Oh, I like your hair.' The woman suddenly stopped scowling and instead beamed. She smoothed her, dazzling blue hair, looked my little girl straight in the eye and said, 'Well, I like your curly hair too.'

The next customer got beamed at too, and who knows, maybe that lady went on to beam at her bus driver, who then went home and hugged his kids, who then...

Do you get my drift? One positive connection can start an awesome chain reaction.

How it works

Recent research has found that in our lifetime we will make connections with about 80,000 people. What an amazing opportunity we have to affect lots of people's lives for the better.

When you smile at someone they usually smile back. Because you make them feel good, they will usually treat you well.

It works the same way with the Earth. When you plant a garden, it will reward you with fruit and flowers.

Activity: Boost your kindness

Write a list of everything respectful or kind you have done today for the Earth and towards other people. What mark would you give yourself out of 10? Make a list again tomorrow and try to better your score.

Create your own calm...

...by giving your respect and kindness to the Earth and to the people who live upon it.

26. Calm at school

A problem is a chance for you to do your best.
- Duke Ellington (Composer and pianist)

If school is something you struggle with you need to try and think about what you can do to make it better. You can often make things better – you don't have to sit around and wait or wish.

It's time to use your problem-solving skills!

It is a good idea to think positive thoughts or do something fun before you tackle a problem. So, get yourself into a good frame of mind first.

How it works

In one study, a group of 4-year-olds were split into two groups. Half were told to think positive thoughts before beginning their block-building puzzles and the other half weren't. Those who thought about happy things finished their puzzles a lot faster and with fewer mistakes than the others.

It is thought that this is because the dopamine that floods our brains when we are happy helps us to learn better too.

Activity: School solutions

We looked at problem-solving earlier in the book, do you remember the 5 steps?

1. Identify your problem
2. explore options
3. make your plan
4. take action
5. reflect (and try again if you need to)

In the activity on the next page, we're going to work through these steps in relation to school.

There are many things YOU can do to help make problems at school better.

For example:

- If you find maths hard you could ask your teacher for extra support, or you can practise at home.

- If you are struggling to make friends, you could join a club at lunchtime or invite someone to your house for tea.

- If you struggle with early mornings, you could prep your school uniform and bag the night before.

Getting help

Some problems are hard to fix yourself though, and it is okay to admit that. When that is the case, knowing who to go to for help is useful.

Make a list of five people you could turn to if you had a problem at school.

First of all, identify what it is about school that is the problem. Is it school work or friendships that worry you? Is it running cross-country or are you being bullied?

Next you need to come up with a plan. One way of coming up with a plan is to mind-map it. Write your problem in the middle of a blank page and shoot off lots of ideas around it. You can ask friends and family for ideas too. It could look something like the drawing on the next page.

Many problem-solving attempts work first time. Sometimes, though, you might need to change your action plan and try again. Keep going till your problem is resolved and do get help if you need to.

PRACTISE BEING ASSERTIVE

STAY AWAY FROM ------

MAKE MY OTHER FRIENDSHIPS STRONGER

------ IS BEING MEAN to ME.

TELL tHE tEAcHER

tEll my PARENtS

Create your own calm...

...by tackling school problems rather than simply worrying about them.

27. Hugging

I love hugging. I wish I was an octopus, so I could hug ten people at a time.

- Drew Barrymore (Actress)

The most important thing to know about hugging is that it is always entirely your choice who you hug. If you are not comfortable hugging someone, you don't need to do it to be polite.

How it works

Scientists have found that when we hug, our brain releases the hormone associated with 'love' called oxytocin. This hormone helps make us feel calmer and reduces levels of the stress hormone (cortisol) in our body.

Hugging also has huge health benefits, protecting us from illness and reducing our blood pressure.

Try a big hug. Research has found that 20 seconds is a great length of time to hug for, to enable all the benefits to start working (but don't worry if that feels too long, just aim for what feels good).

Activity: Hugging practice

Sometimes those we want to hug just aren't around, but we can still get our hugs in and they can still feel awesome! Give these activities a go and give them a mark out of 10 on the feel-good factor when you have tried them.

1 Fling your arms wide then wrap them around your body. Give yourself a gentle squeeze, close your eyes and rock gently from side to side.   /10

2 Lie on your bed and give your pillow a good cuddle.   /10

3 Give a tree a hug and try to feel your connection with nature.   /10

4 Send a hug via a letter or a virtual hug by text to someone you care about.   /10

5 Give your pet (or a teddy bear) a big, long cuddle.   /10

Create your own calm...

...by giving yourself or someone else a good hug.

28. Gratitude

Gratitude is happiness doubled by wonder.
                    - GK Cheston (Literary critic)

What are you grateful for?

Think about five fabulous things in your life you are grateful for and write them in the stars on the opposite page.

How it works

Expressing gratitude doesn't just make us feel good – it has a direct effect on the amount of stress in our bodies. Researchers in California found that people who were taught to be more grateful had a 23 percent reduction in cortisol (the stress hormone) in their bodies. Gratitude is a speedy, simple and proven way to reduce stress!

Activity: Express your gratitude

Try and think about gratitude as a muscle and give it daily exercise to make it strong. Why not have a go at writing a letter to someone you care about, telling them why you are grateful for them?

Create your own calm...

...by making gratitude something you feel every day.

29. Pet therapy

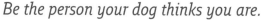

Be the person your dog thinks you are.

— Unknown

Pets can make you feel good in so many ways. Some pets encourage you to sit still and relax as you stroke or cuddle them. Some pets encourage you to get out and about and get exercise and fresh air as you take them for a walk.

Pets teach you to be responsible, nurturing and kind. They can make you feel wanted and needed. They can distract you from anything that might be worrying you.

And all the love you give to them – they give right back.

A pet doesn't have to be a dog or a cat. Even watching fish in a tank can help reduce any muscle tension in your body and lower your pulse rate, to help you feel less stressed.

What if you don't have a pet?

If you don't have a pet of your own, you can still get your pet therapy fix in a different way:

- Offer to walk your friend's dog with them.
- Volunteer to feed your friend's guinea pig whilst they are on holiday.
- Visit/help out at an animal rescue centre.
- Offer to look after the school hamster in the holidays.
- Set up a bird or butterfly feeder in your garden or build an insect hotel.

How it works

Scientific studies have proved again and again how good pets are for both our physical and mental health.

In experiments, where people had to put their hands in ice water or do maths, they were found to be less stressed if they had their pets with them (rather than a friend).

How it works

We asked 5 young people how their pet helped them feel calm. Here's what they had to say:

- 🐾 Milo (aged 8), 'Maggie is my dog and she makes me feel calm when she licks me after I've come out the shower.'

- 🐾 Jamie (aged 9), 'My dog Loki plays with me when my brothers don't and it makes me calm and happy.'

- 🐾 Mack (aged 12), 'Our cat Pixie is so relaxing, she's so loving and cute and she enjoys being stroked.'

- 🐾 Erin (aged 9), 'If someone's been mean to me, playing with Lily, my dog, gets my mind off it.'

- 🐾 Ruby (aged 11), 'My dog Delilah sometimes sleeps on my bed, and cuddling her helps me get to sleep.'

Activity: Anagrams

We've looked at all the things pets can do to help you feel calmer but like all relationships it goes two ways. Can you unscramble the 10 words below to work out what pets might need from you?

REWAT

DOFO

USECDDL

YALP

DBE

MINGGORO

DMEICIEN

SKAWL

PTAEINEC

EOVL

Create your own calm...

...with a little pet therapy.

It is always the simple that produces the marvellous.
                        - Amelia Barr (British novelist)

Life can get so busy and full with activities and school work, clubs and hobbies that sometimes it can leave you feeling tired, overwhelmed and a bit out of sorts.

Slowing life down when you feel like this can really help.

This section has some tips to help you reset, recharge and get back on track by making space for more simple things.

Keeping things simple won't be boring I promise – simple times are often the very best of times.

simplicity

30. Mindfulness

Be where you are, otherwise you will miss your life.
— Buddha

Sometimes we are so busy worrying about what happened yesterday and fretting about what might happen tomorrow that we forget to focus on, and enjoy, today. Mindfulness is about making sure you are fully focused on the here and now.

You might feel mindful when you are watching an ant, painting, singing, looking at the stars or splashing in the sea.

How it works

Lots of research projects have shown that mindfulness is brilliant at reducing stress, anxiety and impulsiveness.

Being mindful calms down the bit of our brain (the amygdala) that make us want to 'fight or flight'.

Because that bit of the brain is calmer, information can go to the part of the brain called the prefrontal cortex instead. This is the part of the brain that helps us make good, sensible choices.

Activity: Mindful activities

Have a go at the activities below and see which ones work for you.

- Run to the end of your street and back, then sit down cross-legged and place your hand on your heart. Sit for a while and feel your heartbeat.

- Eat a small snack quietly, slowly focusing on and appreciating each mouthful of food.

- Blow bubbles slowly, and focus on how they grow, float and eventually pop.

- Have a shower and pay close attention to how the water feels on your skin.

- Take a mindful walk, being aware of all the colours and textures, sights and smells of nature as you do.

Create your own calm...

...by learning to focus on what's happening right now and letting your mind be still.

31. From clutter to calm

Have nothing in your house that you do not know to be useful or believe to be beautiful.
- William Morris (Textile designer)

Physical clutter is all the stuff on your bedroom floor that needs sorting, throwing out or storing away. It is difficult to feel calm when you have stuff everywhere. Just looking at it can make you feel frustrated and cross.

How it works

According to a study by scientists at Princeton University, clutter overloads our visual brain with information and stops us thinking clearly. Other studies have found it can make us feel worried, miserable, tired and sad.

You will need three bags: one for gifting, one for giving to charity, and one for recycling.

1. Look through your books and see if there are any to take back to the library, then gift, give or keep the rest.

2. Go through your clothes, taking out anything that doesn't fit or that you no longer like. Decide whether to gift, give or recycle.

3. Declutter your pencil case/desk. If the pens have dried up and rubbers have worn out it is time to ditch them.

4. Now let's move on to puzzles, games and toys – there is no point keeping anything incomplete so put that into the recycling. Games and cuddly toys you have outgrown can go straight into the giveaway/charity shop bag.

5. Treasures may include card collections, trophies or certificates, or perhaps much-loved teddies. You may decide to display them or you may want them safely stored.

Create your own calm…

…by keeping your space clear and organised.

32. Simple and speedy calm hacks

The more simple we are, the more complete we become.
- François-Auguste-René Rodin (Sculptor)

There are lots of very simple things you can do to keep yourself feeling peaceful.

Knowing how to be calm when you need to is such a powerful skill to learn, so it is well worth practising over and over till you get good at it.

Why don't you have a go at the ideas in these clouds and see what works best for you?

Brush your teeth and wash your face for an instant refresh

Lay on your back with your eyes closed, and let your body relax

Do something to help someone (it will make you and them feel happier)

Count to 10 slowly, then back down to 1. You can't stay upset when you are counting

Go for a walk somewhere lovely

Go to a happy place in your mind. Maybe a beach you love or your Grandma's kitchen table.

Tell someone how you feel

Fuel your body with a cold drink and a healthy snack

Write down how you feel

Look in the mirror and say, 'I am calm and in control'

Have a good shake to release muscle tension

Push your palms together for ten seconds

Play your favourite song and have a quick disco

Stamp your feet and blow out your breath to help you feel grounded

Get some fresh air to cool you down

Create your own calm...

...by becoming an expert calmer-downer.

33. Being Un-busy

Make it simple but significant.

- Anonymous

Doing something simple can be wonderful.

Playing cards with your family in a small caravan could bring you more pleasure than 3 hours on a games console with all your mates and a pile of sweets.

I know that might sound hard to believe.

Busy can be fun but too much busy can make our brains ache. It's important to make time for simple things.

How it works

Scientific research has found that letting our minds wander can boost how creative we are in our thinking; and that playing games and taking walks help with that too.

Just think, a bit of time pottering about and you could end up writing the next bestseller!

Activity: Un-busy yourself

Here are some slow and simple ideas that are perfect for your down time. Tick off the ones you try...

Nurture a plant

Fly a kite

Play an instrument

Phone your grandparents

Make a butterfly feeder

Play monopoly

Make shortbread

Peel an orange and take in the scent

Make a paper aeroplane

Offer to wash the car

Turn off your TV

Take photographs

Create your own calm...

...by making space for the simple things in life.

Creativity is inventing, experimenting, growing, taking risks, breaking rules, making mistakes, and having fun.

- Mary Lou Cook (Actress)

Being creative can help you relax, increase your self-esteem, and it can make you feel more confident and capable. And it is lots of fun!

Being creative is for everyone – no skill required. All you need is a willingness to have a go and let go of the idea of perfection.

In this section, we will look at lots of ways to be creative and all the many benefits that being creative brings.

CREATIVITY

34. Music

*Life seems to go on without effort when
I am filled with music.*

- George Eliot (Author)

Did you know that music affects your brainwave speed? Fast, lively music can make you feel energized and upbeat. Slow, rhythmic music works like meditation and can make you feel relaxed.

How it works

In a hospital, researchers found that patients who listened to music whilst having an operation had lower levels of the stress hormone (cortisol) in their bodies compared to patients who didn't listen to music.

What a simple way to reduce your stress!

Music directly affects the chemicals released in your body too. Loud music gives us a shot of adrenaline which make us feel awake. Calm, classical music reduces our 'alertness chemicals' and can help with getting to sleep.

Do you have an emotional reaction to music?

Activity: Become a music detective

Try listening to lots of different kinds of music. Write down next to each type of music how the song made you feel. What kinds of music make you feel the calmest?

Nature sounds

Jazz

Classical

Pop

Country

Rock

Disco

Heavy metal

Lullabies

R + B

Punk

Create your own calm...

...by using music to change your mood.

35. A collage of calm

Stressed is desserts spelt backwards.

- Unknown

The things that make me feel peaceful will often not be the same things that make you feel peaceful. Everyone is unique and has their own life story that shapes who they are and what they feel. Discovering what makes you feel peaceful and filling your life with more of it is one of the most important things you can ever do for yourself.

What are your top 5?

How it works

In 1922 the scientist Albert Einstein jotted down his thoughts on happiness on some hotel stationery in Tokyo. He wrote:

'A calm and humble life will bring more happiness than the pursuit of success and the constant restlessness that comes with it.'

If the world's greatest scientist thought the secret to happiness was being calm, then it must be worth focusing on!

Activity: Create a collage of calm

Have a go at making a collage of things that make you feel peaceful. You can write or cut out words, draw pictures, stick on photos or fabrics or anything else you like. Be as creative as you wish.

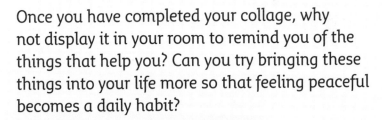

You will need:

- Paper/Card (as big as you want)
- Colouring pens
- Glue
- A few old magazines/newspapers you can cut up
- Any other bits and bobs you like

Once you have completed your collage, why not display it in your room to remind you of the things that help you? Can you try bringing these things into your life more so that feeling peaceful becomes a daily habit?

Create your own calm…

…by focusing on what makes you feel more peaceful.

36. Create a relaxation jar

Actions seems to follow feeling, but really actions and feeling go together.

- William James (Psychologist)

Taking time to relax is a brilliant way to help your mind and body switch off from pressures you might feel from home, school or friends.

Doing something to help yourself feel better (even when you don't feel like it) will give you back a sense of control.

How it works

Scientists believe that relaxation should be at the top of everyone's to-do list. They say it reduces wear and tear on the mind and body in so many ways.

They found that when we relax, the flow of blood increases around the body, giving us more energy. It also helps us to have a calmer and clearer mind, which helps us to think more positively and make decisions more easily.

Relaxation ideas

You could try some of the following ideas:

Now come up with some brilliant ideas of your own to fill the speech bubbles on the next page.

Activity: Make a relaxation jar

It can be tricky to think of ways to relax when you aren't FEELING very relaxed. Feeling tense impacts our ability to take action and make choices. That's why we need to make this list of relaxation options BEFORE we feel all tense – so let's have a go at doing this, by creating a relaxation jar.

Take all the ideas you have listed opposite, add a few more and write each one on blank lollipop sticks or small bits of coloured paper that you then fold into squares.

Decorate a jar with glass pens or stickers or a label saying 'relax' and pop your ideas inside.

When you feel tense and just don't know what to do with yourself, grab an idea at random from your jar and just 'do it'. You won't have to think about it, or make choices – you will simply be presented with an activity to help you relax.

Create your own calm...

...by regularly taking time to relax.

37. Colouring mandalas

Colour is a power which directly influences the soul.

- Wassily Kandinsky (Russian abstract artist)

Colouring can take your mind off your worries and help it relax. Studies have shown that patterned circles known as mandalas are especially good for you to colour. People who colour mandalas often experience a deep sense of calm and wellbeing.

A mandala is a spiritual symbol in the religions of Hinduism and Buddhism, and represents the universe. In these religions, it is believed that mandalas have special healing powers.

There are some wonderful things worth knowing about mandala colouring:

- Mandala means circle.
- There is no right or wrong way to colour a mandala.
- You can colour just about anywhere.
- You can colour at your own pace.
- You don't have to follow any rules when you colour.
- You know you're creating a unique work of art.
- It can feel deeply relaxing.

How it works

Scientific studies show that colouring a mandala has the same effect as meditation. The shapes and patterns of mandala designs need a lot of concentration which can help us distance ourselves from feelings of stress and anxiety.

Activity: Colouring your mandala

When colouring, try not to think too much about your choice of colour and don't worry about matching colours. Let your instincts guide you.

If choosing colours is something you normally struggle with, just pick four colours at the start and put the rest of them away. This takes away the choice-making, so you can truly relax.

Here are some lovely pieces of music you could listen to while you colour in:

- Nocturnes by Chopin
- Clair De Lune by Debussy
- Für Elise by Beethoven
- Swan Lake by Tchaikovsky

Before you say 'AAAGH no!' to this music, just try listening to it whilst you colour your mandala. THEN decide what you think.

Create your own calm...

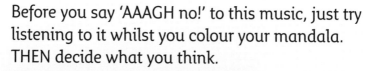

...by giving new things a try and keeping an open mind, it can bring such wonderful things into your life.

colour me

38. Making bread

Good things come to those who bake.

- Unknown

Baking bread will make all your senses happy. For a start, kneading bread feels fantastic. You can absolutely bash it about and get rid of any tension you may feel. Plus, bread smells delicious as it bakes and watching bread rise is fascinating.

How it works

Did you know the smell of freshly baked bread is often used in supermarkets to encourage shoppers to spend more?

Scientists think the smell brings back lots of lovely memories and makes people think of family, childhood and comfort, which makes them happy.

Activity: A super simple bread recipe

You will need:
- 3 cups strong bread flour
- Pinch of salt
- 1 packet of quick action yeast
- 2 tablespoons of vegetable oil
- 1 cup of warm water
- 1 tablespoon of sugar

Recipe:

- First off, preheat the oven to 200°C (or 180°C for a fan-assisted oven).
- Add the dry ingredients to a bowl and mix well.
- Make a well in the middle and add in the oil and warm water.
- Stir the mix until it comes together, then turn out onto a lightly floured surface and knead.
- Knead the dough for 5–10 minutes until it is smooth.
- Once the dough is kneaded, make into shapes that you want and put in a warm place to double in size – this takes around an hour.
- Bake for 15–20 minutes for rolls, 20–30 minutes for loaves. The bread should sound hollow when tapped. Leave on a wire rack to cool.

Thanks to 'Rainy Day Mum' blog for permission to use this recipe.

Create your own calm...

...by getting your bake on.

39. Calm colours

*Colour! What a deep and mysterious language,
the language of dreams.*

- Paul Gauguin (Artist)

Our brains link colours to our memories, so when we see a colour we immediately 'feel' it because of what we remember.

Bright colours may make us excited as we think of parties and fairgrounds, and natural colours may make us relaxed as we recall walking through the woods or paddling in the sea.

How it works

Scientists have discovered that we often link a colour back to how we see it in nature. Blues and greens might remind us of water, sky, fields and trees, and so generally those colours relax us. Red might remind us of fire, and scare or excite us.

- Blue has been shown to make people feel calm, a useful colour if you are feeling stressed.

- Violet (a kind of purple) is said to bring inner peace and wisdom.

- Yellow is the colour of sunshine – brilliant for lightening and brightening your mood.

- Green is all about balance and peace – wonderful for helping you feel more Zen.

- Pink is the colour of gentleness and caring – ideal when you need to be kind to yourself.

- White is the colour of freshness and it is believed to help you have clear thoughts.

Activity: Colour investigation

Splodge lots of colours that you THINK make you feel relaxed onto a piece of paper.

Come back to it later and look with fresh eyes at the colours – which ones make you feel the calmest?

Can you make a list of ideas to bring more of these colours into your world?

Create your own calm...

...by using colour to change your mood.

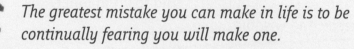

40. Worry dolls

The greatest mistake you can make in life is to be continually fearing you will make one.

- Elbert Hubbard (Philosopher)

Worry dolls were created many years ago by the Mayan people in Guatemala. The idea was that, when someone had a problem that would stop them from sleeping, they would tell each of their worries to one of the dolls. Then they would put the dolls under their pillow, and the dolls would 'worry' for them during the night, and they could sleep peacefully and wake up feeling a whole lot better.

Nowadays children all over the world have their own little bags of tiny worry dolls they tell their cares to at night and pop under the pillow.

In talking to your worry dolls, you are putting your thoughts and feelings into words. Naming your concerns helps you make sense of what is troubling you. Having a clearer mind, emptied of worries, will help you sleep.

How it works

Psychologists at a university in California found that talking about and labelling feelings makes them less intense. They did a study that got people to attach feeling words such as 'fear' and 'anger' to faces they saw in photos.

When they did this, it showed up in brain imaging that they were a lot less upset than when they looked at the photos without naming the feelings.

Giving a label to the feelings they could see helped their brains to relax.

Activity: Make your own worry dolls

You will need:
- Wooden dolly pegs
- Coloured string, twine or wool
- Felt-tipped pens
- Glue stick

Making your own dolls can help you feel attached to them and is a lot of fun.

All you have to do is wrap your wool around the peg's body to look like clothes. Using different colours makes the doll look more traditional. When you are done, draw a little face on with your pens. You could stick on some wool for the hair.

They will be a little bigger than traditional worry dolls but just as cute.

The dolls might feel a bit lumpy under your pillow so you could given them their own little cover and place them somewhere close to where you sleep.

As long as you tell them your worries before bedtime, they will still do their job.

Create your own calm...

...by emptying your head of worries before you go to sleep.

The root of all health is in the brain. The trunk of it is in emotion. The branches and leaves are the body. The flower of health blooms when all parts work together.
- Kurdish saying

Our minds and bodies are completely linked. When we are stressed, frightened or worried, signals whizz all around our bodies preparing them to fight or run.

One way to stop this is the relaxation response, which was developed by a heart doctor called Herbert Benson. He believes people should practise relaxation every day so that they have a more peaceful mind and better health.

This section will give you lots of brilliant tools to help you switch on the relaxation response and take control of your own calm.

MIND
&
BODY

41. Exercise

You're only one workout away from a good mood.
                                        - Unknown

The very best time to exercise is when you least feel like it.

Here are some of the brilliant benefits that exercise can bring:

- Exercise is distracting. It's hard to think about things that are wrong whilst you are chasing a tennis ball or running a race.

- Exercise can make you more confident – the more you do it, the more you will get better at it.

- Getting fit will help you feel good about yourself as you will feel stronger and more capable.

- Playing a sport with other people can be fun and a great way to make new friendships.

- Regular exercise can boost your mood and help you sleep better.

How it works

NHS guidelines say that children from 5 to 18 should do at least 60 minutes of moderate-intensity exercise every day. Moderate intensity means your heartbeat gets faster and you breathe harder.

Exercise has been shown to increase levels of serotonin, which increases levels of happiness and wellbeing. Exercise releases endorphins, which are the feel-good chemicals that act on the brain to calm us down and help with mood swings.

Activity: Find your exercise

If you haven't found anything you like yet, then have a go at something new. Circle the ones you've tried below:

Bike-riding

Rowing

Karate

Running

Aerobics

Swimming

Gymnastics

Playing frisbee

Skipping

Skateboarding

Ice skating

Walking

Tennis

Roller skating

Rugby

Horse-riding

Trampolining

Badminton

Football

Dancing

Create your own calm...

...by making sure you get lots of exercise!

42. Belly breathing

*When the breath wanders the mind also is unsteady.
But when the breath is calmed the mind too will be still.*
- Svatmarama (Author)

When you are fearful, angry, or feeling uptight it affects your body. Your muscles will tense up and your breathing becomes shallower. When your breathing is shallow, it is hard to think clearly.

Taking long deep breaths enables your body and your mind to become calmer.

How it works

Researchers at Stanford University School of Medicine found there are 175 brain cells which pay close attention to what our breath is doing and, as a result, make alterations to the state of our mind.

The neurons which link breathing to relaxation, attention, excitement and anxiety are embedded in our brains and they pick up on our breathing.

Activity: How to belly breathe

Lie flat on the floor on your back and place both hands on your stomach.

Breathe in and out through your nose. Begin to inhale deep breaths into your tummy until you feel your tummy inflating like a balloon. You will feel your fingertips begin to separate and join back together again as you breathe out.

Make your exhale (breath out) long and slow so that your tummy button moves back towards your spine.

As you breathe in, you might like to repeat to yourself, 'I am' and as you exhale finish the sentence with something positive, like 'calm', 'strong', 'happy'.

Belly breathing is great for aiding relaxation, so doing it before bed is good or else at times of tension, such as exam time.

Create your own calm...

...by breathing deeply and switching on your relaxation response in your body and mind.

43. Even more brilliant breathing exercises

Breathing is the greatest pleasure in life.
       - Giovanni Papini (Writer and philosopher)

By looking after your body, you can help your mind relax. By looking after your mind, you can help your body relax. It is a powerful circle of calm you can control.

Here are some more great breathing techniques to practise.

Bee breathing

Another fun breathing exercise is to put your hands on your ears and inhale through your nose as if you are smelling a flower. Then breathe out whilst making a buzzing bee sound. You can play around with this by making long noises, short noises, whatever works!

Blowing out the candles

Hold your hands up in front of your face with your palms facing you. You are going to pretend that your fingers and thumbs are all candles. Inhale through your nose then blow your breath out slowly through pursed lips, blowing out that first candle. Then inhale through your nose and exhale slowly and blow out that second candle, and so on until all ten candles are out.

Feather breaths

Place a feather on a table. Breathe in through your nose for a count of 3, hold your breath for 3 then slowly breathe out through your mouth trying to blow the feather as far as you can across the table.

Simply breathing

If you are somewhere public and you don't fancy making bee sounds or blowing on your fingers you can simply try this:

- Breathe in through your nose whilst counting slowly to 3.
- Then, without pausing or holding your breath, breathe out to the count of 4.
- Repeat until you feel relaxed.

Create your own calm...

...by breathing through times of stress until it passes.

44. Yoga

You cannot always control what goes on outside.
But you can always control what goes on inside.
        - Wayne Dyer (Motivational speaker)

Yoga works on your body and mind and can bring you a great deal of peace. It has been practised for thousands of years.

How it works

Our nervous system connects our brain to our body and sends lots of messages rushing between the two.

One branch is called the sympathetic nervous system. This increases our heart rate, blood pressure, stress levels, and tension in our muscles.

Another branch is called the parasympathetic nervous system and it does exactly the opposite. It helps us relax. It lowers our heart rate, blood pressure, cortisol (stress) levels and muscle tension.

Completely releasing all muscular tension is one of the best ways to calm the nervous system, which is one of the reasons why yoga is so healing.

Activity: Child's pose (Balasana)

Yoga teacher Donna Navarro shares a simple yoga exercise called child's pose or *Balasana* (bah-LAHS-uh-nuh).

The child's pose helps you feel calm, rested and stable and is a wonderful yoga pose to help you sleep too.

1. Begin on all fours.
2. Bring your knees wider and your big toes together.
3. Bring your bottom back to sit on your heels and as you breathe out, lengthen forward to bring your forehead to the floor.
4. Lengthen your arms out in front of you, resting them along the floor.
5. As you breathe in, feel the top of your back expand and as you breathe out feel your ribs draw closer together.
6. Focusing on your breath will help to still your mind and calm your nervous system.
7. Do this once for 1–3 minutes.

Create your own calm...

...by practising a little yoga on a regular basis.

45. Guided meditation

The quieter you become, the more you can hear.

– Unknown

You can meditate in lots of different ways, such as breathing, mindfulness and yoga. One really lovely way to meditate is with a guided meditation.

Because of the way the mind and body are connected, you can totally feel like you are experiencing something deeply relaxing just by imagining it. Isn't that amazing?

Lie down and close your eyes and have someone read you 'The flying boat ride' and see how relaxed it makes you feel.

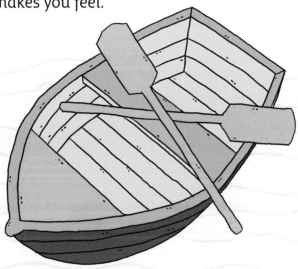

The flying boat ride

Close your eyes gently and take in a few slow, deep breaths.

I am going to count from 5 down to 1 – when I get to 1 you will feel calm and deeply relaxed.

5   **4**   **3**   2   1

Imagine a beautiful pathway leading down a sloping hill. You are barefoot and the grass beneath you feels soft and damp. As you walk slowly down the pathway, the sun is warm on your face and you feel content.

You see a beautiful lake. You kneel down when you reach it and run your hands through the turquoise waters. It is as warm as a bath.

You see a little wooden boat bobbing gently at the water's edge. You climb in and the boat feels steady and secure beneath you.

Your body feels strong as you take the oars and row out onto the lake. The water is perfectly still.

You feel the boat rise slowly at the front and begin to leave the water. It tips you only slightly and you firmly hold the sides as you look with awe as it rises, heading towards the clouds.

Soon you are in the sky and you notice your boat now has oars made of beautiful golden feathers.

You feel totally safe and snug on your little boat. Looking down you see the shimmering lake, the emerald green grassy hills and a few tiny houses. A gentle breeze ruffles your hair.

You let go of any worries. You feel nothing but awe and wonder and deep joy as your boat gently flies you over our beautiful Earth. You are far above anything that has been bothering you and it all seems so small.

How powerful you are as you row steadily through the clouds.

Slowly you direct your little boat back to the lake and with your strong arms you steadily row your boat back to the shore.

You say thank you to the boat as you climb out of it and lay the oars gently back inside. You can come back to your boat any time you like and take another magical journey. It's always there for you, ready to take you far from your worries.

Breathe in deeply and exhale slowly.

Breathe in all the happiness and wonder from your boat ride and keep them with you.

You've done a wonderful job relaxing and imagining.

When you're ready, give your body a big stretch and gently open your eyes.

Create your own calm...

...by taking a ride in your imaginary boat whenever you need to.

46. Self-massage

Time you enjoy wasting is not wasted time.
- Unknown

It is important to take some time each day to be kind to yourself and to fill yourself up with feelings of calm and wellbeing.

How it works

The benefits of massage are pretty amazing. Scientific studies have shown that hand massage not only has physical benefits but also that it causes:

- reduced anxiety
- a better mood
- improved sleep

Activity: Self-hand massage

Before you begin:

- It is important to make sure you are in a relaxing environment.
- Concentrate on breathing in through your nose to the count of 7, and out through your mouth to a count of 7 for a little while first.
- Use a pea-sized amount of baby oil.

The massage:

- Gently and slowly rub the oil into your hands.

- Roll your wrists in circles, 5 times to the left and 5 times to the right, repeating for each of your hands.

- Pinch your fingertips using your thumb and index finger and repeat on both hands.

- Make a tight fist then fully open your hand. Repeat this 5 times for each hand.

- On each finger, rub in the oil using circular motions from your palm to your fingertips, repeating this for both hands.

- Next, massage circular movements from the base to the top of your palm 5 times on each of your hands.

- Lace your fingers together and push them away from your body to stretch your fingers and wrists apart.

Thanks to Natalie Johnson for her super-relaxing hand and wrist massage.

Create your own calm...

...by learning to self-massage.

47. PMR

PMR stands for progressive muscle relaxation and don't worry, it's nowhere near as complicated as it sounds.

PMR is a simple and helpful way you can remove stress by tensing your muscles then relaxing them.

How it works

A doctor called Edmund Jacobson created PMR in the 1930s as he believed physical relaxation helped calm his patients' minds.

Muscle tension is often caused by stress and anxiety. When you tense your muscles then let go of the tension your muscles relax.

Relaxed muscles require less oxygen so your breathing calms down too. Your heart rate also calms down. Soon your mood calms down in response to your body. It's hard to feel anxious when your body is relaxed.

Find a space to sit or lie down and get comfortable. You are going to make the muscles around your body relax. Each time, you are going to tighten your muscles as you breathe in for a count of 8, then you are going to quickly relax them and breathe out:

1. First scrunch up your face. Breathe in whilst you do this. Then breathe out and let your face relax as if you were sleeping

2. Next tense your shoulders (shrug them) and relax

3. Now work down your body...
   - Pull in your tummy and release.
   - Ball your hands into fists then let go.
   - Tighten your leg muscles then release.
   - Scrunch your toes up then relax.

You can do this as quickly or as slowly as you like, but the longer you take the more deeply relaxed you will feel.

Create your own calm...

...by practising PMR several times a week – get so used to it you can easily use it if you are feeling tense.

48. Anchors

When you're feeling anxious, remember that you're still you. You are not your anxiety.
- Deanne Repich (Founder and director of the National Institute of Anxiety and Stress)

This section may feel a bit complicated at first so you might want your grown-up to work through it with you.

What do anchors do?

Anchors are used to moor a ship to the bottom of the sea and help make it secure. The anchors we are going to talk about do just the same job except not for a ship, these anchors are for you – to help you feel calmer when life seems stormy.

People often respond without thinking to things that are familiar. For example, certain smells such as warm apple pie may make you feel warm and safe because they remind you of your Grandma's house.

Anchors are the experiences – the sounds, sights, feelings, smells or tastes – which lead automatically to a particular response.

How it works

The idea of using an anchor to change how you feel is often used by therapists.

Anchoring occurs when we do two (unrelated) things together over and over again, enough times for the brain to link the two together. We are PURPOSEFULLY connecting two activities together in order to cause an automatic response.

For example, if we imagine feeling super confident and say the word POW, and repeatedly practise this, then eventually just saying the word POW may trigger feelings of confidence within us.

colour me!

Activity: Setting your calm anchor

You can set your own anchors to help you feel calmer.

Here is how to do it:

1. Make sure you are feeling calm, perhaps sit quietly colouring or reading for a few minutes. Let yourself relax.

2. When you are feeling relaxed slowly open and stretch wide the fingers of one of your hands. Do this 5 times while saying to yourself, 'I feel calm' as you do it.

3. To develop an anchor that works, you should do it frequently. Try and get into a calm state of mind and set your anchor 5 times every day for a week. You can tick it off on the chart opposite when you have done it.

4. Soon, you can simply flex your fingers and say in your head, 'I feel calm' and it should take you back to that feeling of being super relaxed.

CALM ANCHOR

	1	2	3	4	5
M Monday					
T Tuesday					
W Wednesday					
T Thursday					
F Friday					
S Saturday					
S Sunday					

5 Of course, you don't have to flex your fingers. Pretty much anything can work as your anchor, such as a word or movement of some kind. You might want to make it something no one else can see so you can do it discreetly.

Create your own calm...

...by setting an anchor to take you to a calm place.

49. Eat Yourself Calm

Good food equals a good mood.

- Unknown

Sometimes when people get too hungry they feel angry. This is called being 'hangry'. It's unpleasant for everyone, including you. You can easily avoid it by making sure you eat regularly and healthily.

According to the NHS, most people in the UK eat and drink too many calories, too much fat and too much sugar and they don't eat enough fruit, vegetables, oily fish or fibre.

It doesn't do our bodies or minds good to eat junk food, according to the NHS. Instead they suggest we eat a regular, balanced and healthy diet.

How it works

Government guidelines show that to have a healthy, balanced diet, people should try to:

- Eat at least 5 portions of a variety of fruit and vegetables every day
- Base meals on higher-fibre starchy foods like potatoes, bread, rice or pasta

- Have some dairy or dairy alternatives (such as soya drinks)
- Eat some beans, pulses, fish, eggs, meat and other proteins
- Choose unsaturated oils and spreads, and only eat them in small amounts
- Drink plenty of fluids (at least 6 to 8 glasses a day)

Calm food choices

Did you know that lots of foods can make you feel calmer? Here are just a few examples. Can you look up some more?

Eggs

Eggs contain an amino acid called tryptophan which helps create serotonin. Serotonin is a chemical in our brains that helps to even out our moods, helps us sleep and decreases anxiety.

Eggs are great scrambled or in an omelette.

Pumpkin seeds

Pumpkin seeds are high in magnesium, zinc and iron. These all help your brain work really well. When your brain is in good health, stress levels can lower too.

Pumpkin seeds are great sprinkled on soup or cereal, or eaten on their own, as a snack.

Spinach

Leafy greens such as spinach also contain magnesium, which can help boost your mood.

Spinach tastes great mixed with salad leaves or on a pizza.

Blueberries

Blueberries are full of vitamin C and other antioxidants, which can improve your brain health and, as a result, help you feel less anxious (all berries are good for you actually!).

Blueberries are great on your cereal.

Bananas

Just like eggs, bananas also contain the amino acid called tryptophan, which makes your body produce serotonin. This raises your spirits and helps reduce stress.

Have a look at the recipe on the opposite page for banana ice cream.

Activity: Banana ice cream

Simply freeze banana chunks for at least 1 hour, then pop into a food processor and whizz until smooth. You can add some regular milk or almond milk to make it smoother if you like.

Once smooth, you could add in any other ingredients you fancy, such as:

- A spoonful of peanut butter
- A handful of blueberries
- A few spoons of dark choc chips

(All super-calming additions!)

Then you simply continue to blend until it's all completely mixed. You can either eat it straight away or pop it into the freezer until it's frozen, then serve when you wish. This isn't the prettiest ice cream, but it is so tasty!

Create your own calm...

...by choosing foods that are good for your brain.

50. Sleep

Doctor, doctor, I have trouble getting to sleep at night. Lie on the edge of the bed – you'll soon drop off.

- Unknown

Did you know that we spend around 25 years of our lives asleep?

Sleep may feel like a bit of a boring thing to do but it is important and impacts your life in lots of ways.

Sleep can affect your mood, your health, your energy levels and your concentration.

How it works

A study at the University of Pennsylvania found that people who slept for only 4½ hours a night reported feeling sad, stressed and bad-tempered. Just as soon as their sleep went back to normal their mood did too.

According to the NHS, this is about the amount of sleep you need each night, depending on your age:

7 years - 10 hours 30 minutes

8 years - 10 hours 15 minutes

9 years - 10 hours

10 years - 9 hours 45 minutes

11 years - 9 hours 30 minutes

12 years - 9 hours 15 minutes

Tips to help you sleep more easily

Try the following tips to improve your sleep:

- Keeping your bedroom dark, quiet and tidy helps your body to rest and relax and produce the sleep hormone melatonin. This makes it much easier for you to fall asleep.

- Whether you write out your worries or talk them over with a grown-up, do try and get them out of your head before you sleep so your mind can relax.

- Going to bed at the same time every night and waking at the same time helps you get into a routine. Try to keep to these times at weekends too so your body doesn't get confused.

- Electronic devices can be great fun but they need to be kept out of the bedroom, with no screen time for at least an hour before bed.

- A regular wind-down routine before bed prompts your body that it's time to sleep.

Activity: Bedtime routine

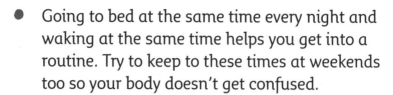

Devise a little bedtime routine for yourself and try to follow it for a week. It might include a warm drink or bath or time to read. Write the order in which you are going to do each activity, and what time you are going to go to bed on the opposite page.

At the end of the week, reflect on how good your sleep has been and if it has improved. Do you feel more relaxed and refreshed in the mornings?

Create your own calm...

...by sleeping well and waking up refreshed.

You can create your own calm by practising the ideas in this book and finding which ones work best for you. Then you will be able to help yourself whenever you need to.

If you do find an activity that you feel works really well you might want to teach it to your friends or your family or even share it with your class – spreading calm into the world is a lovely thing to do.

Your emotional health and wellbeing is every bit as important as your physical health so be sure to take care of it by giving yourself the love, relaxation, peace and nurturing you need.

colour me!

Go forth and...

cREAte YouR OWN calm